Everything You Need to Know About

Cults

This prayer room was used by Swedish cult members for a mass suicide.

Everything You Need to Know About

Cults

Sean Dolan

The Rosen Publishing Group, Inc.
New York

To Clementine, who always shows a mind of her own.

Published in 2000 by The Rosen Publishing Group, Inc.
29 East 21st Street, New York, NY 10010

Library of Congress Cataloging-in-Publication Data

Dolan, Sean.
    Everything you need to know about cults / Sean Dolan.
        p. cm. — (The need to know library)
    Includes bibliographical references and index.
    ISBN 0-8239-3230-3 (lib. bdg.)
        1. Cults. I. Title. II. Series.
BP603 .D65 2000
291.9—dc21
                                                                00-020959

Manufactured in the United States of America

Contents

The Branch Davidians of Waco, Texas, were involved in a long-term standoff with U.S. law enforcement officials.

Chapter One

Myth or Menace?

Cults may not be the first thing that comes to mind when you think of important issues for teens. Yeah, sure, everyone has probably heard the more sensational stories: the cult in Japan that released poison gas in the Tokyo subway system; the group in California that committed mass suicide so they could join the mothership somewhere in outer space beyond the Hale-Bopp comet; the group in Waco, Texas, whose living space was burned down—with members inside—after a weeks-long armed standoff against U.S. law enforcement officials.

But how relevant to everyday life are these groups? The people in these cults were clearly nuts—mentally ill or emotionally disturbed—right? Many people believe that people who belong to cults are freaks or weirdos, religious zealots, or social outsiders who are not particularly intelligent or well-educated and are easily manipulated. Most people also think that there was probably something a little wrong with these cult members long before they even joined a cult; otherwise they would not have been interested in belonging to such a group in the first place. Another common belief is that cult members were not mentally strong enough to recognize and resist the persuasion techniques that cult members supposedly use to convince others to join.

You may even have heard that cults use "brainwashing" or "mind control" to gain recruits and keep members. To some people, the idea sounds ridiculous. *Brainwashing? Isn't that something that happens to soldiers captured in battle and prisoners held in dungeons by evil dictators?* If you are like most people, you're pretty sure that no one you know, including yourself, would be interested in joining a cult. Or would be vulnerable to whatever recruiting techniques a cult may use. Or dumb enough to be fooled by such techniques.

You're probably right—about some of this stuff, at least. Even if the highest estimates for the number of cults and cult members in the United States today are correct, it is still true that the average young person is unlikely to have his or her life affected in any significant way by cult activities. Other issues, such as violence in the home and in schools, probably—and rightly—seem more immediate and important. Most teens deal with questions concerning substance use and sexual behavior more often than they do issues related to cults. A teen in the United States today is more likely to know an adult afflicted with some form of cancer than he or she is to know a cult member. A teen is at greater risk of contracting a sexually trans- mitted disease (STD), of being the victim of a violent crime, or of being involved in an automobile accident than he or she is of being successfully recruited or seduced by a cult.

Even so, there is much that can be learned from observing and examining the cult phenomenon. And this information relates to issues—questions of reli- gion, individual freedom and civil liberties, leadership and power, group dynamics, communications and the power of persuasion—that are of great importance to all members of society.

Chapter Two

What Is a Cult and What Do Cults Do?

The People's Temple incident is still the most famous—and probably the most disturbing—of the various tragic stories involving cults that have made headlines in the last thirty years.

The first news reports about the incident were vague and not taken very seriously, probably because the events described seemed so unbelievable. In mid-November 1978, a small group led by Congressman Leo Ryan of California flew to Guyana, a small nation in South America, to investigate troubling reports about a religious group known as the People's Temple.

According to relatives and friends of members of the People's Temple, various forms of physical and mental coercion—the act of forcing someone to do something or behave in a certain way against his or her will—were

Jim Jones amassed a huge and loyal following for his People's Temple.

being used to keep members from leaving the group. Critics charged that the People's Temple was more of a cult than a religious organization.

The People's Temple had a relatively long history for such a group. It had been founded in Indianapolis, Indiana, in 1953 by the Reverend Jim Jones, a twenty-two-year-old Methodist preacher. At the time, Jones had a strong commitment to social justice, especially equal rights for African Americans. First in Indianapolis and then in the California cities of Ukiah, San Francisco, and Los Angeles, where Jones established new branches of his church, the People's Temple earned a reputation for doing good work with some of those cities' poorest citizens, especially racial minorities, drug addicts, and the homeless.

The People's Temple set up soup kitchens, day care centers for children, and medical clinics for the elderly. It also established programs that provided counseling to prostitutes and drug addicts and helped them change their lives. In San Francisco especially, the People's Temple was regarded by many as an excellent example of the kind of positive social changes that a small, committed organization could help bring about. By the 1970s, Jones was so well regarded as a public figure that he was named chairman of the San Francisco Housing Authority.

By that time, however, there were already signs that something was drastically wrong within the People's Temple. The few people who succeeded in leaving the group told disturbing stories. Jones's behavior, they said, was becoming increasingly unpredictable and upsetting. He had long since left the Methodist Church and now seemed to consider himself the new Messiah, a holy man sent by God to save the world from the wickedness that was spreading through it.

Jones declared this belief during frequent long, angry speeches, which were driven by his constant use of amphetamines (a type of illegal drug that acts as a stimulant, or upper). Jones claimed that the outside world was trying to destroy his church and its members. Meanwhile, former members told of beatings and other forms of abuse within the group, and relatives of those in the group insisted that the members of the

People's Temple were being forced to remain in the group against their will.

Such reports sparked new interest in the group among journalists, law enforcement officials, and politicians. Jones insisted that this interest was evidence of a plot by Satan to destroy the group. When reporters discovered more proof of what was going on within the group, including evidence of horrendous child abuse, Jones moved the church and its members—more than 800 in all—to Guyana, where land was cheap and the local government was not particularly interested in his activities.

Jones had promised his followers that Guyana would be a tropical paradise, but the reality was far different. "The moment I got off that plane I knew something was wrong," said Richard Clark, a former member of the People's Temple. Clark ran away, but the other members of the group were put to work building a primitive compound, which they named Jonestown, in the steamy jungle. Everyone, including children, worked from seven in the morning until six in the evening, six days a week, in temperatures often as hot as 100 degrees Fahrenheit. On the seventh day, members of the People's Temple were subjected to Jones's endless sermons, in which he spoke angrily about the forces plotting against the group.

Not paying attention during a speech was a very serious offense. For example, parents who whispered a few words to each other while Jones was speaking were punished through their children, who were made to perform sexual acts in front of the group.

In general, children were the victims of most of Jones's abuse. Parents were forced to surrender care of their children to the group as a whole, and Jones was addressed by all as Dad. Children were allowed to see their parents only briefly at night. Teenagers performed more than half the backbreaking work of building Jonestown. Children who "misbehaved"—by becoming too tired to work, for example—were punished by being made to spend the night at the bottom of a well. Beatings were common, as was torture with electric shocks. Members who were considered serious disciplinary problems were kept for weeks in a plywood box that measured six feet by four feet by three feet, and those who tried to run away had a ball and chain attached to their ankle. Guards patrolled the compound day and night to ensure that Jones's orders were followed.

This was the situation when Congressman Ryan arrived in Guyana in November 1978. Although Jones greeted the Ryan party warmly and showed them around Jonestown as if he had nothing to hide, it was clear that the visit worried him. In the weeks leading up to Ryan's arrival, Jones insisted on frequent rehearsals of what he called White Night—a mass suicide by all group members to be committed when it became clear that the People's Temple could no longer hold out against its enemies.

For Jones, Ryan's visit was the sign that the end was near. When Jones learned that some of his followers had asked Ryan for help, telling the congressman that they wished to leave Jonestown but believed that they would be killed if they tried, Jones panicked. When Ryan's delegation returned to its two planes, Jones's guards began shooting, killing Ryan and four others and disabling one of the planes. The rest of Ryan's party got away in the other plane, carrying with them film footage of the attack.

That footage was the first news story about Jonestown seen by the outside world. It took the Guyanese army a day to cut its way through the jungle to the compound. What the soldiers discovered was difficult for the world to believe. The first reports, which told of 100 people dead, were disturbing enough, but the reports that followed were even more horrifying. Almost all of the members of the People's Temple at Jonestown were dead. In the mud at Jonestown, Guyanese soldiers found 912 bodies, including Jones's and 278 corpses of children. The vast majority of the victims, on Jones's orders, had drunk a fruit punch mixture laced with cyanide, a deadly poison. Adults had fed the poisoned liquid to the children, including infants. Those who had tried to disobey Jones's orders had been shot.

Faith or Force?

The Jonestown tragedy did more than any other single event to change the public's awareness and understanding of cults. What was most difficult for many people to understand was how the members of the People's Temple had been persuaded or coerced into acting against some of the most basic human instincts—self-preservation and the protection of loved ones, particularly children.

Especially puzzling was the fact that much of the evidence indicated that the great majority of the members of the People's Temple had died by drinking the poisoned punch—that is, they seemed to have killed themselves by choice. But why hadn't more of them tried to run away or resist, particularly when it came to saving their children? Jones had always claimed that all of his group's actions were motivated by religious beliefs, but many people refused to believe that any kind of religious conviction, no matter how misguided, could account for what had happened at Jonestown. They argued that although many of the people at Jonestown might have seemed to have willingly committed suicide, something had happened to them—or had been done to them—that affected their free will and ability to make healthy, independent decisions.

The Unification Church

At approximately the same time, several other events were making Americans increasingly aware of cult activities. By the late 1970s, the Unification Church, a quasi-religious organization founded by the Reverend Sun Myung Moon, a businessman and former

More than 1,000 people died in the mass suicide of People's Temple members in Jonestown, Guyana.

Presbyterian clergyman from South Korea, claimed a following of 30,000 members in the United States. Moon called himself a Christian, but his church was devoted primarily to what he called his Divine Principles, which emphasized anti-Communism and the approaching coming of a new Messiah, who was said to be Moon himself.

Although the church's actual membership in the United States was probably much smaller than its claimed figure, it was able to amass considerable wealth and purchase a large amount of real estate and several businesses, including the *Washington Times*, a daily newspaper in the nation's capital. (The Unification Church still owns the *Washington Times*, which in the 1980s President Ronald Reagan called his favorite newspaper.)

Most of the church's new members were young people. These Moonies, as they were sometimes insultingly referred to, became a familiar sight in many of the nation's cities, where they became notorious for their unusual fund-raising techniques, such as selling flowers and trinkets in the roughest neighborhoods, seemingly twenty-four hours a day.

People were even more puzzled by the huge group weddings carried out by the church, sometimes in sports arenas, in which hundreds and even thousands of couples were married at the same time. The marriages had all been prearranged by the Reverend Moon; in many cases husband and wife met each other for the first time at the ceremony. Immediately after the ceremony, many of the couples were split up, again on the church's orders, with spouses sent to different areas of the country and even the world to do the church's work—primarily the recruitment of new members.

Although no event involving the Unification Church was as dramatic or tragic as what occurred at Jonestown, similar charges concerning its activities were made, particularly by parents whose children had become involved with the group. The Moonies, such critics claimed, were somehow being influenced to act against their own free will and often against their own best interests. Without evidence of physical force being used to gain and keep new members, critics found it difficult to detail and prove exactly how this was being done, but they remained certain of it.

Sun Myung Moon, considered by some to be the Messiah, at one time had more than 30,000 followers in the United States.

Religious Belief or Mind Control?

Friends and relatives of people who had joined the Moonies and similar groups, which by that time were being referred to as cults, echoed many of the same complaints. They claimed that their loved ones had turned into completely different people, cutting off contact with friends and family, giving up old hobbies and activities, and devoting almost all of their time and energy to the new group. To outsiders, the cult members seemed as if they were hypnotized or in a trance. Their thought processes appeared to be slowed down, they gave automatic responses to questions, and it was difficult to have a conversation with them on any topic besides the cult and its teachings.

Observers claimed that they could detect a strange or faraway look in the eyes of cult members.

Defenders of the Unification Church and similar groups offered a different explanation: Members of these groups were in fact different from the way they had been, but the changes were the result of genuine religious conversion (a change in belief or faith). Leaders of these groups often used Biblical references to explain the transformations. A common example was Christ's instructions that if a person wishes to be saved, his old self must "die" and be born anew, and he must "sell all he owns and follow me." Another common defense was to point out that throughout history, believers in new religious or political groups had often seemed strange or unusual to outsiders and had often been persecuted just for being different.

Patty Hearst and the SLA

Another event that occurred around the same time provided a different interpretation. In 1974, Patricia Hearst, the nineteen-year-old heiress (inheritor) of one of the country's wealthiest and most famous families, was kidnapped by the Symbionese Liberation Army (SLA), a small radical political group. The group, which was dedicated to revolutionary violence, was already wanted for the murder of the superintendent of schools in Oakland, California.

Newspaper heiress Patty Hearst was kidnapped by the SLA and eventually sympathized with her captors.

Within two months of the kidnapping, the SLA released tape recordings in which Hearst was heard declaring that she had been converted to the SLA's way of thinking and now considered herself a revolutionary. She had even changed her name to Tania. A short time later, Hearst was photographed carrying an automatic weapon and participating in a bank robbery with the SLA. For months afterward she stayed with the group as it tried to elude a nationwide manhunt. Even after three of its members were killed in a shootout with law enforcement officers and despite having a number of opportunities to escape, Hearst remained with the SLA.

When the last remaining members of the SLA were captured, Hearst was among them. At her trial for the crimes she had committed while with the SLA, Hearst's lawyer, the famous F. Lee Bailey, offered an unusual and creative defense. Through a combination of physical and psychological abuse, Bailey argued, Hearst had been brainwashed into behaving the way that the SLA demanded. Although the jury did not fully agree, the judge seemed somewhat sympathetic. Hearst was convicted for participating in the SLA's crimes, but she received a surprisingly light sentence.

For many people, the concept of brainwashing seemed to offer an explanation for the personality changes and unusual behavior that were beginning to be associated with cults. Others used different terms to explain the same phenomenon—"coercive persuasion" and "mind control" were the most commonly used.

So What Is a Cult?

According to the most traditional definition, a cult is simply religious belief or worship, or the people or group that engages in such worship or faith. Over time, the word has come to be used to refer to groups that hold beliefs or engage in practices that are generally regarded as unorthodox or illegitimate (illegal or not accepted by society). Most often these groups are primarily religious in focus, but cults can also be political in nature or devoted to practicing an alternative, or different, lifestyle from that of mainstream society.

Historically, cults have often been offshoots or splinter groups that break away from larger, more established organizations. Some of the oldest of these cults eventually became so large and powerful that they could no longer be considered cults. For example, historians of early Christianity frequently write about the "Jesus cult" or "Jesus movement" that sprang up within Judaism in the first century AD, following the death of the individual known to history as Jesus Christ. One of the questions that these historians have long attempted to answer is how this movement, which was extremely small at first and was persecuted by the authorities, succeeded in such a relatively short time— no more than a couple of centuries—in becoming the dominant religion within the Roman Empire. Obviously, by the time it achieved this success, it was no longer a cult but the religion known today as Christianity. Today very few people could refer to Christianity as a cult and expect to be taken seriously.

Defenders of modern cults argue that groups today should be understood with this history in mind. They point out that the United States began as a haven (safe place) for religious groups that were persecuted elsewhere. Using the examples of the early Christians, as well as such groups as the Quakers, Puritans, and Catholics that came to the New World to escape religious

For several centuries following the death of Jesus Christ, his followers were persecuted as cult members.

persecution in their homelands, they argue that "one person's cult is another person's religion."

But others argue that the traditional definition of a cult must be updated to address the reality of today's cults. According to this updated definition, a cult is based less on what its members believe, the size of the group, and its relationship to the larger society than on what it does—specifically, on what it does to recruit, convert, and keep members.

Chapter Three

Understanding Cults Today

For many who have studied cults, the actions of Aum Shinrikyo and Heaven's Gate—two cults that have received enormous media attention in the past several years—are further proof of the accuracy of the new understanding of cults that has developed in the years since Jonestown.

Aum Shinrikyo

On March 20, 1995, Aum Shinrikyo, a Japanese cult, released a deadly nerve gas called sarin into the crowded subways of the city of Tokyo at rush hour. The fumes overcame hundreds of riders, sending many to the hospital and killing twelve. The cult had been known to Japanese authorities for many years, but the

In 1995, the Aum Shinrikyo cult released a deadly nerve gas into Tokyo's subways at rush hour, killing twelve people.

government had been unable to act upon various charges of assault, kidnapping, and other activities made against the group because Aum Shinrikyo had received legal standing as a religious organization in 1989. Aum Shinrikyo's legal status in Japan meant that the government was legally forbidden to investigate the group's religious activities or doctrine.

After the attack, the Japanese police and military rounded up more than 400 members of the cult, including its leader, a blind, charismatic former yoga teacher named Shoko Asahara. In the process they learned much about the cult, its teachings, and its plans. Amazingly, Asahara had succeeded in recruiting a number of talented and well-educated professionals, including several doctors and scientists, with his teachings, which were a mixture of Buddhist and Shinto principles and quasi-scientific theories. Asahara's goal was to use his group to bring about Armageddon—the great battle that would mark the end of the world. At that point, Asahara believed, only he and his followers would be left. To achieve that goal, the group had developed the ability to produce large quantities of sarin gas and was studying methods to release it in urban areas to create the maximum amount of suffering and terror.

Heaven's Gate

Almost two years later to the day, in Rancho Mirage, California, police uncovered another horrifying example of the devastating power of cults. In a luxurious house in this suburb of San Diego, police found thirty-nine dead bodies, all dressed in jumpsuit-like uniforms and shrouded in purple. Each of the thirty-nine had committed suicide by swallowing poison. Medical examinations revealed that many of the men had, at some earlier date, castrated themselves.

Among the dead was Marshall Herf Applewhite. Applewhite, who called himself Do (pronounced "dough"), was the sixty-six-year-old leader of a group known as Heaven's Gate. The bodies found with him were his followers, who believed him to be the reincarnation (modern-day form) of Jesus. The group had

The Heaven's Gate cult members wanted to join powerful beings in space to achieve salvation.

formed in the mid-1970s and was dedicated to the belief that a small group of select human beings had been chosen for salvation by powerful beings from outer space. For more than twenty years, the members of Heaven's Gate had been waiting for the arrival of an alien spacecraft that would take them up into space.

In early 1997, Applewhite interpreted the discovery of the Hale-Bopp comet and its close orbit to Earth as signals of the arrival of the spaceship. Applewhite convinced his followers that in order to join the beings in space, they would have to shed their bodies—in other words, die. The deaths of his followers—the largest such mass suicide in U.S. history—was the result.

One Definition: Actions, Not Beliefs

Most observers of present-day cults would agree with the definition of cults offered by Dr. Michael Langone, a psychologist who has written extensively on cults. According to Langone, a cult is a small group or movement that has five crucial defining characteristics. It must:

- ♦ Demonstrate a great or excessive devotion or dedication to some person, idea, or thing
- ♦ Use some form of thought control to gain and keep members
- ♦ Create a state of psychological dependency in members
- ♦ Exploit members of the group to attain the goals of the leaders
- ♦ Cause psychological harm to members, their families, and the outside community

You will notice that this definition of a cult contains no references to what a cult believes. That is because according to experts like Langone, the content of a cult's belief is less important than the methods the cult uses to convince its members to believe in its message and to act accordingly. For example, what made the Heaven's Gate group a cult was not its belief that its members were to reach salvation with the help of

29

aliens—no matter how ridiculous or unlikely this idea sounds to outsiders. After all, millions of people around the world consider the fundamental doctrines of the Catholic Church to be irrational (against common sense and reason). These people find it hard to believe that Jesus is the son of God, that he was born from a virgin, or that he rose from the dead. Even so, very few people would seriously argue that the Catholic Church is a cult.

What makes a group a cult, according to Langone and others, is not the irrationality or acceptability of what it believes, but the manipulative nature of the methods it uses to get its members to believe and participate in cult activities. Experts also point out that cults vary in the degree to which all five elements are reflected in the group's activities. They refer to this as the totality of the cult experience.

Likewise, the size of the group or the degree of its acceptance by mainstream society is not really important in determining whether or not it is a cult. Both the Unification Church and Aum Shinrikyo were recognized as legitimate religious organizations by the legal systems in the United States and Japan, which gave them various tax and legal benefits. For Aum Shinrikyo, legal recognition meant that the government was not allowed to investigate its religious activities or doctrine. This is what enabled the group to escape scrutiny (careful investigation) until after its attack on the Tokyo subway system.

Types of Cults

This newer definition means that, at least in theory, a cult can form around almost any kind of belief system. The nature of these beliefs determines the type of cult. Steven Hassan, a psychologist and exit counselor—someone who helps former cult members after they leave their group—believes that cults today in the United States fall into four main categories:

- Religious cults
- Political cults
- Psychotherapy/Educational cults
- Commercial cults

Let's examine these categories in more detail.

Religious Cults

Many of the groups that have been discussed in this book so far—the People's Temple, the Unification Church, Aum Shinrikyo, and Heaven's Gate—fall under the category of religious cults. The hallmark (main characteristic) of a religious cult is excessive attention to spiritual issues. Most religious cults emphasize the corruption, or rottenness, of the material world and the purity of the cult. This purity is maintained by the group's withdrawal from the world and immersion in the life of the cult.

Some cult members believe that salvation will arrive through otherworldly forces, such as UFOs.

Often the cult's teachings take on an apocalyptic tone—that is, they emphasize the upcoming end of the world, or the second coming of Jesus Christ. Often the group's teachings include some of the beliefs of mainstream religion, but emphasize the special role to be played by the cult in carrying out divine prophecy. In other cases, as with Heaven's Gate, salvation is to be achieved not in any traditional religious sense but through the intervention of otherworldly forces or beings, such as UFOs or aliens. In many cases, the cult's leader claims to be a prophet or guide who receives divine messages about the future and holds the key to the group's salvation.

Political Cults

The Symbionese Liberation Army is an example of a political cult. Political cults tend to emphasize the reform (change) of society, sometimes through violent means. Once again, the leader of the group is often believed to possess special insight and abilities that are vital to the cult's success. Similar to religious cults, political cults often emphasize the corruption of the larger society, although they look to political action rather than spiritual redemption for answers. Some cults, such as the People's Temple, take on aspects of both spiritual and political cults.

Psychotherapy/Educational Cults

Psychotherapy/educational cults often disguise themselves as self-help groups. Such cults can take a variety of forms. Virtually every form of teaching or therapy that promises individuals greater insight, self-esteem, spiritual power, inner peace, physical or psychological health, or financial or romantic success has been used by cults to attract and keep members. Psychotherapy, meditation, and yoga are just three examples of potentially positive tools for learning and awareness that have been abused in a dangerous way by cults. Such groups often promise their members more and more important insights and secrets as they advance within the group. Advancement requires paying for increasingly expensive special lessons or seminars that are supposedly offered only to the most worthy students.

Commercial Cults

Commercial cults promise their members riches, usually through the sale of a specific special product. In many cases, what the cult is actually selling is itself. The cult often functions as little more than a pyramid scheme, meaning that it makes money essentially by continually gaining new members, who are charged various fees for the right to sell the cult's products. Potential converts are promised a lucrative (financially successful) future selling the product. In reality, however, the convert most often winds up turning over whatever money he or she earns to the group, while also feeling constant pressure to recruit new members.

Thought Control

It is worth repeating that the nature of a group's thoughts or beliefs is not what makes a group a cult. Belonging to a group that believes that the second coming of Christ is near does not automatically make you a member of a cult. Likewise, there is nothing inherently cultish about yoga, meditation, psychotherapy, or door-to-door sales of laundry detergent. In fact, religious belief, political commitment, and the desire for self-improvement are used by cult leaders to make their groups seem legitimate precisely because these feelings and impulses are genuinely worthy, among the best of human characteristics. What can make the cult experience so difficult to understand, and ultimately so tragic and destructive, is that a cult often takes advantage of the very best qualities of its members, who truly believe in the group's idealistic message.

What all of today's cults have in common is the use of manipulation to gain and keep members and to serve the leaders' interests. Experts use different terms to characterize this manipulation. At the time of Patty Hearst's capture by the SLA, "brainwashing" was the term used most often. Brainwashing was also used by many as a possible explanation for the events at Jonestown. More recently, experts have preferred other terms, such as "coercive persuasion," "mind control," or "thought control."

Brainwashing

The concept of brainwashing first became familiar to the American public in the early 1950s. At that time, the United States was fighting a war in Korea against troops from the Communist nations of North Korea and the People's Republic of China. "Brainwashing" emerged as a term to explain certain behavior that Americans found difficult to understand, such as why captured U.S. servicemen gave public denunciations (announcements of their rejection) of their country to the North Koreans. Brainwashing was believed to be a combination of techniques—torture, intimidation, indoctrination, hypnosis, and sleep and food deprivation—that left the subject unable to think for him- or herself and extremely susceptible (vulnerable) to suggestion. The concept of brainwashing became even more widespread with the success of the 1961 movie *The Manchurian Candidate,* in which an American prisoner of war during the Korean War is released after having been brainwashed and programmed to assassinate a popular American politician upon his return to the United States.

In time, brainwashing, at least of the kind portrayed in *The Manchurian Candidate,* came to be seen as a kind of science fiction. To date, there is no reliable evidence that a person such as the assassin in *The Manchurian Candidate* can be programmed to act in a certain way. However, there is much evidence of the effectiveness of certain techniques, often used in combination, to influence thought and behavior and compromise free will. Robert Jay Lifton, a prominent psychologist, prefers the term "thought reform."

How Does Thought Control Work?

Although some people still consider the idea of thought control far-fetched, there are a number of examples that are probably familiar to most people. The example of prisoners of war giving statements in support of the enemy is a common one. Anyone who works in the legal system knows that it is not uncommon for suspects to be persuaded to confess to crimes that they did not commit. Psychologists have conducted several experiments

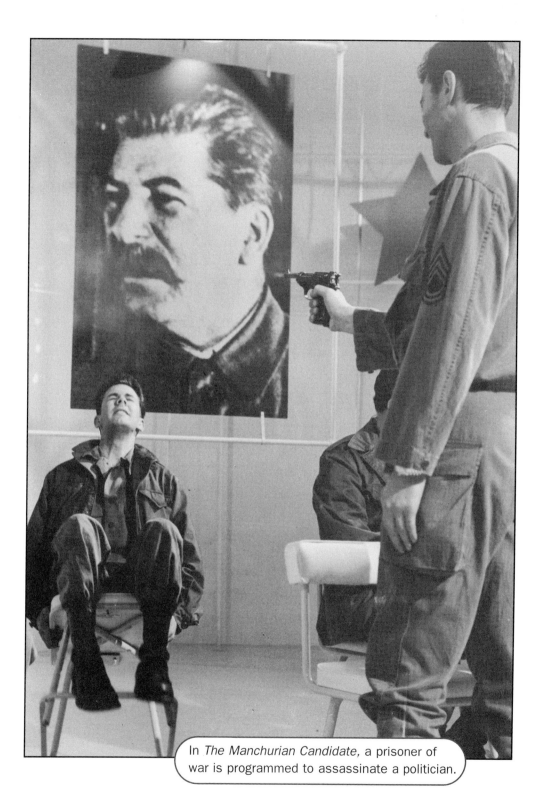

In *The Manchurian Candidate*, a prisoner of war is programmed to assassinate a politician.

that demonstrate how easily individuals can be influenced by an authority figure to conform to (go along with) the behavior of a group, even when that behavior goes against their own beliefs. In a famous experiment conducted by psychologist Stanley Milgram at Yale University, a surprisingly high percentage of subjects were willing to administer what they thought was a form of torture to a stranger rather than disobey the spoken commands of an authority figure.

Short-Term Control

What motivates an extreme type of conformist behavior is relatively easy to understand. In the case of the prisoner of war, fear and isolation, combined with physical and psychological abuse, possibly even torture, and lack of food and sleep can very easily combine to persuade someone to say or do whatever the captor wants. Likewise, fear, isolation, and various forms of deprivation, along with sometimes just the threat of physical abuse, have often been used to convince innocent people to confess to crimes that they did not commit.

In these instances, it can be argued that what has taken place is not really a form of thought control. Instead, the subject of the coercion has agreed to say or do something in order to end some kind of abuse or stress—to stop being tortured, for example. The Milgram experiment at Yale is slightly different. In that case, the authority figure had no real power over the subject. He did not physically harm the subjects, mentally abuse them, or hold them in captivity. Yet the fact that he presented himself as an authority figure was enough to convince most people to go along with his commands, even when by doing so the subjects believed that they were causing another human being great physical pain.

A somewhat less dramatic example, called the Asch experiment, demonstrates a similar point. In the Asch experiment, the subject is placed in a room with a number of strangers. The strangers are actually confederates—people working with the researcher to run the experiment. The subject, however, has no idea that he or she is the only person in the room who doesn't know the purpose of the experiment.

Each person in the room is then given an identical piece of paper showing two lines, one of which is clearly longer than the other. The subject is then asked to identify which line is longer. What the subject does not know is that the confederates have been instructed to claim that the shorter line is in fact the longer one. The point of the experiment is to observe how much persuasion it takes to convince the subject to change his or her answers to go along with the group, even when the group's answer clearly contradicts what the subject knows to be correct or true. What the Asch experiment and variations on it have shown is that most subjects give in very easily to peer pressure and are quickly persuaded to go along with what the group says is correct.

Long-Term Control

All of the examples previously described shed some light on how cults practice mind control. However, in each of these examples the degree of persuasion is relatively minor and brief in duration. A suspect or captive might make a false confession to end the ordeal of interrogation (questioning), but once that ordeal is over, he or she is unlikely to continue admitting to the crime. The threat of physical coercion in particular tends to be short-lived. Physical force can be an extremely effective way of persuading a person to do or say something, but once the threat of physical punishment is removed, the persuasive effect often disappears as well.

Likewise, once the subjects in the Asch experiment are removed from the group setting, their confidence in their own judgment tends to return quickly. In the Milgram experiment, too, it was the environment in which the experiment was conducted and the presence of the authority figure that created the persuasive effect.

In all of these cases, some form of persuasion has clearly taken place, but not necessarily thought or mind reform. Observers would not detect signs of complete personality changes, in contrast to what observers of cult behavior find—and what former members of cults describe. Cult members are not just saying, doing, or professing to believe something in order to avoid some negative consequence. For all intents and purposes, they believe in the cult's teachings, and their actions reflect these beliefs—but neither the beliefs nor the actions reflect their individual free will.

How do cults accomplish this? Although experts disagree over some of the details, they agree that cults succeed by exercising complete control over a person's environment in order to leave the individual isolated, fearful, dependent, and confused. In this state, the person is bombarded with what is presented as the answer to that stress, confusion, fear, and loneliness—namely, the group's message. Once the individual makes a tentative commitment to the cult, these techniques are intensified until the new member's commitment solidifies.

At that point, time works in favor of the cult. The more a person has invested in a cult—in terms of things such as time, money, and emotions—the more unlikely it is that he or she will be able to do what it takes to leave. By that point, the typical cult member will have surrendered so much of his or her previous life—friends, family, romantic relationships, education, work and career, money, years of a life—that it becomes that much more difficult to admit to having been manipulated or tricked.

Chapter Four

The Process

Contrary to popular belief, most people who join cults in the United States are not outcasts or marginal members of society. Nor is there a greater incidence of mental or emotional problems among them than in the population at large. Studies have shown that cult members tend to be slightly better educated than average and no poorer than average. In general, experts do not believe that there is any class or type of person that is more or less vulnerable to indoctrination by cults. Indeed, some experts maintain that, under the right circumstances, *anyone* is susceptible to the type of persuasion that cults practice.

Who Gets Recruited?

What most people who join cults have in common is that the initial contact with the group comes at a time

Tom Cruise is a member of the Church of Scientology, which has often been accused of being a cult.

of transition, vulnerability, or stress. Many of those who join cults are young adults, and their contact with the cult comes soon after they have left home and are living on their own for the first time. This is a time of emotional vulnerability for many young people. The aftermath of a romantic breakup is another time at which young people may be particularly vulnerable to a cult's approach. For this reason, many cults recruit on and around college campuses.

Young people are also frequent targets of cults because they are often idealistic. The desire to make a difference in the world, to bring about social change, to gain spiritual insight and wisdom, or to improve one-self are ideals shared by many young people. It is

John Travolta is another high-profile celebrity who is a member of the Church of Scientology.

people with these goals and ideals that cults are most successful at appealing to.

How Does Recruitment Work?

A cult's initial approach to a potential recruit is usually cleverly hidden. Obviously, when approaching a potential new member, recruiters do not announce that they are part of a cult. If they are members of a group that is well known, they are likely to be vague about the name of the group, or may even give false identification.

Often the approach is made in person. In other cases, cults hand out flyers and handbills advertising seminars, lessons, religious instruction, or sometimes just a social gathering without giving any detailed information about the identity or nature of the cult. In some cases, however, the group is straightforward about its identity. The Church of Scientology, for example, has often been criticized for being a cult, but it maintains a very high public profile through advertising and its association with a number of celebrities, including Tom Cruise and John Travolta.

"Love Bombing"

The initial approach is intended to lure the recruit to a group gathering. These gatherings usually take place over an extended period of time in a setting—a church, a house in the country, a campground or retreat—away from the recruit's usual environment.

Once the recruit is present, the group concentrates on getting him or her to relax, mainly by making him or her as comfortable as possible. One way of doing this is by giving the recruit an enormous amount of positive attention. The Moonies call this love bombing, and many cults practice some variation of it. The idea is to get the recruits to let down their defenses and relax their powers of critical thinking by convincing them that they are in a nonthreatening environment filled with friendly, gentle, kind people who share the recruits' interest in spiritual matters, social reform, and political dedication. At first, the cult's pitch is focused less on a hard sell of its message than on making the recruit comfortable with the other members of the group. The focus will often be on showing that the other members of the group are "normal" people who are "just like" the recruit.

Increasing Commitment

As the recruit shows more interest in the group, such gatherings may become more frequent, longer, and more intense. At the same time, the recruit will be pressured, sometimes very subtly, to demonstrate an ever-increasing commitment to the cult. As this occurs, the cult slowly increases its control over the new member and his or her environment. He or she will be encouraged to limit contact with outsiders, particularly friends and family members. As the recruit begins to accept the "truth" of the cult's message, such requirements start to seem less like unreasonable demands than the natural result of following such an inspiring message. People who have succeeded in leaving a cult report that at the time of their recruitment, they were largely unaware of the extent to which they had been cut off from previous social contacts.

Isolation

Cults usually limit other outside influences as well, such as television, radio, books, and movies. This is often easier than it may sound. One way is to keep the recruits constantly occupied, more or less around the clock, with cult activities, leaving them with no time for anything else. It also makes them too exhausted to think critically about their situation. The cult's teaching reinforces this isolation by creating an "us against them" mentality regarding the outside world. Within the world of the cult itself, social contact is usually strictly regulated. Members are often encouraged to live communally (as a group) in a setting controlled by the cult, where all conversation and social interaction can be monitored and controlled.

Within a short time recruits find themselves in a setting where they are essentially bombarded nonstop with only the information that the cult wants them to receive. Having cut themselves off from family, friends, school, and employment, recruits find themselves emotionally, socially, financially, and spiritually dependent on the cult. If you consider that the cult's message is always that it alone possesses the secret to salvation, social change, financial success, self-improvement, or spiritual fulfillment—happiness, in short—it becomes much easier to understand why the cruder forms of coercion and control, such as physical violence or intimidation, are rarely necessary for cults to keep their members in line. The cult member simply comes to feel that he or she has no life to return to outside the cult.

Cults as Moneymakers

There is nothing wrong with devoting your life to your beliefs, of course. But life for most cult members becomes endless days working for the cult, usually as a fund-raiser. The early methods of the Unification Church, in which members raised money by selling flowers and asking for donations, have since been replaced with more sophisticated tactics. Applewhite's followers in Heaven's Gate, for example, were all

trained to make money working as computer programmers and technicians. They earned good salaries but
turned almost all of their money over to the group.
Likewise, the followers of Frederick Lenz, a self-styled
guru with a nationwide following in the 1980s and 1990s,
earned money as computer programmers. They would be
kept awake and stimulated during marathon work ses-
sions with Jolt Cola and Ho-Hos provided by the cult.
While Lenz lived in a huge mansion on luxurious
grounds on Long Island's North Shore, his followers lived
in cheap communal housing, turning their paychecks
over to the group. Similarly, the Reverend Sun Myung
Moon has become enormously wealthy as a result of the
efforts of the members of the Unification Church.

In this way, manipulation by the cult becomes the
oldest trick in the book—a financial con (trick) by
which the leaders of the cult enrich themselves at the
expense of their followers. In other groups, such as
the People's Temple and the Branch Davidians, the
leaders are interested less in wealth than in power and
prestige, but the methods they use are the same. In
some instances cult leaders may actually believe their
own teachings.

Exits: Leaving a Cult

Leaving a cult, or exiting, can be extremely difficult,
but no method of coercive persuasion is foolproof or
100 percent effective over time. In fact, experts

believe that most cult members eventually leave. These exits fall into three categories: walkaways, castaways, and interventions.

Walkaways

The vast majority of cult exits are walkaways. A walkaway is just what it sounds like: The cult member simply decides to leave the group. As we have seen, no method of thought reform is totally effective, and walkaways are often the result of emotional and physical burnout as much as a conscious rejection of the cult and its teachings. Most walkaways simply sneak away from the cult in the middle of the night.

Castaways

Castaways are members that the cult asks to leave, either because of suspicions about their reliability and commitment or, more often, because they are no longer of use to the group as recruiters, workers, or fundraisers. Members who become physically or mentally ill because of the stress and isolation of cult life often become castaways.

Interventions

An intervention is an exit that takes place because an outsider takes some action to persuade the member to leave. Most often this outsider is someone paid by the family of the cult member to "rescue" him or her. In the past, such people called themselves deprogrammers.

Teens who leave cults benefit greatly from the support of exit counselors.

Their interventions were known as deprogrammings, and they took the form of a forcible removal of the member from the group and enforced isolation at some secret site. There, usually over a period of several days, the cult member would be bombarded with information, often in a threatening manner, to persuade him or her to leave the group. The idea was to use some of the more intense methods of coercive persuasion to undo the programming the member was believed to have undergone within the cult.

One problem with deprogramming is that it is not very effective, and its success is often limited to the short term. Once the person is removed from the coercive setting of the deprogramming, he or she will often return to the cult. Another major problem is that it is illegal. Even if you believe that someone you care about has fallen under the influence of a cult, you cannot capture and hold the person without his or her consent, even for a short period of time. The law considers this kidnapping.

Exit Counseling

Today interventions most often take the form of what is known as exit counseling. An exit counselor is a professional employed by family or friends to intervene with a cult member. Exit counselors frequently are former cult members; many of them, such as Steven Hassan, have received formal training as counselors, therapists, or psychologists. Working with the family, exit counselors try to convince the cult member to meet with them. If successful, they then present the cult member with as much information as possible about the cult, its practices, and the ways in which the person's thoughts and decisions may have been manipulated.

In many cases, exit counselors draw on their own experiences with cults to establish a bond with the member. This information is presented in a nonthreatening manner, with the intention of breaking through the cult's hold of isolation and enabling the member to begin thinking for him- or herself once again.

The Challenges of Exiting

Overall, exit counseling has been much more effective than deprogramming. Exit counseling has also been helpful for castaways and walkaways. Leaving a cult is

It can be very difficult to resume a normal life once you have left a cult.

just the first step on what can be a long and painful road to recovery. Former cult members face a number of difficulties in reconstructing their lives after leaving the cult. Here are some of the challenges that exiting members face:

- Family relationships have to be repaired, as do friendships. In some cases, the harm done to such relationships may be irreparable.

- Resuming a career or an education can be difficult, and it can be hard explaining your time in a cult to a potential employer or admissions counselor who wants to know what you have been doing with your life for the past several years.

- Recent exit members often experience feelings of stress and frustration, anger at being manipulated, and guilt about the hurt done to friends and family as well as about those still left in the cult. In addition, as relieved as cult members often are to be out of the group, they often experience a great sense of sadness about the loss of something that once gave such great meaning to their life. The result can be severe depression and related problems that make it hard to resume a normal life. Exit counseling can be very effective in addressing such problems.

Chapter Five

Triumph of Will

Perhaps you still do not believe everything the experts say about cults. Maybe you don't believe that you, or anyone, could fall victim to a cult and some form of coercive persuasion. It could never happen to me or someone I know, you might think. You might not even think that mind control or thought reform is a real thing or an adequate explanation for what goes on in cults. Some people would agree with you.

Even so, the Cult Awareness Network estimates that at this moment there are more than 2,000 groups in operation in the United States that qualify as cults. One prominent researcher believes that more than four million Americans have been involved with cults since the late 1960s. A study conducted by the prominent psychologist Philip Zimbardo in the mid-1980s indicated that 3 percent of high school students in and around one major American city (San Francisco) had engaged in cult activity, and more than half of the students surveyed reported knowing a fellow student who was involved with a cult.

Of course, most cult members do not wind up committing mass suicide, participating in group marriages, running from the FBI, or shooting it out with federal law enforcement agencies. Most may not give up their life savings or a family inheritance to the group. But although less dramatic, the harm done to their lives is no less real or significant.

Perhaps one of the saddest aspects of the cult phenomenon is the damage it does to the ideas of faith, belief, and commitment. When such qualities are so manipulated, it can be easy to become cynical and to regard any kind of belief as misguided, fraudulent, or corrupt.

But that would be tragic. The ability to believe is one of humanity's greatest gifts, just as the freedom to choose what to believe is one of humanity's fundamental rights. The abuse of that freedom, like the abuse of any fundamental freedom, is a crime.

Glossary

brainwashing A forcible indoctrination to make someone give up basic political, social, or religious beliefs and to accept other very rigid ideas.

castaway A member of a cult who is asked by the group to leave. Most castaways are members who have lost their effectiveness, either because of sickness or exhaustion, and have thus become a burden to the cult.

coercion The act of compelling someone to make a choice or act in a certain way, often by force or the threat of its use.

coercive persuasion A variety of techniques used by cults to control or instill certain kinds of behavior and beliefs in their members. Other similar terms include "thought control," "mind control," "thought reform," "mind reform," and "brainwashing."

deprogramming An outmoded and often illegal technique used to convince cult members to leave the group. Deprogramming often took the form of forcible removal from the group, a period of captivity in the control of the deprogrammer, and a barrage of anticult propaganda.

exit counselor A professional who is specially trained in helping individuals deal with the problems associated with leaving cults and rejoining mainstream society.

immerse To plunge into something that surrounds or covers.

indoctrinate To influence another person very strongly with a specific idea, opinion, or point of view.

intervention An action by a concerned individual or individuals to influence a person's awareness of the consequences of his or her self-destructive behavior and to help him or her change that behavior.

susceptible Open, vulnerable, or nonresistant to an influence.

walkaway A cult member who decides on his or her own to leave the group and does so, often simply by sneaking away in the middle of the night. Most people who leave cults are walkaways. Walkaways prove that cult efforts at thought control are almost always less than total.

zealot A fanatic; someone who is extremely devoted to a religion or a set of beliefs.

Where to Go for Help

In the United States

American Family Foundation
P.O. Box 336
Weston, MA 02193

Cult Awareness Network
2421 West Pratt Boulevard, Suite 1173
Chicago, IL 60645
(312) 267-7777

Interfaith Coalition of Concern About Cults
111 West 40th Street
New York, NY 10018
(212) 983-4977

International Cult Education Program
P.O. Box 1232, Gracie Station
New York, NY 10028
(212) 439-1550

Jewish Board of Family and Children's Services
Cult Clinic Service
1651 Third Avenue
New York, NY 10028
(212) 860-8533

Unbound
P.O. Box 1963
Iowa City, IA 52244
(319) 337-3723

Wellspring Retreat and Resource Center
P.O. Box 67
Albany, OH 45710
(614) 698-6277

In Canada

Council on Mind Abuse
Box 575, Station Z
Toronto, ON M5N 2Z6

Info-Cult
5655 Park Avenue, Suite 305
Montreal, PQ H2V 4H2
(514) 845-6756

For Further Reading

Cohen, Daniel. *Cults*. Brookfield, CT: Millbrook Press, 1994.

Hassan, Steven. *Combatting Mind Control*. Rochester, VT: Park Street Press, 1990.

Langone, Michael, ed. *Recovery from Cults: Help for Victims of Psychological and Spiritual Abuse*. New York: Norton, 1995.

Singer, Margaret Thaler, with Janja Lalich. *Cults in Our Midst: The Hidden Menace in Our Everyday Lives*. San Francisco, CA: Jossey-Bass, 1995.

Zeinert, Karen. *Cults (Issues in Focus)*. Springfield, NJ: Enslow Publishers, 1997.

Index

Index

About the Author

Sean Dolan lives and works in New York. He has written many books for young adults.

Photo Credits

Cover and pp. 2, 6, 23, 26, 32 © Archive Photos; pp. 11, 17, 19, 21, 28 © Corbis; pp. 37, 43, 44 © The Everett Collection; pp. 50, 52 by Thaddeus Harden.

Design and Layout

Michael J.Caroleo